D0399230

The smallest feline is a masterpiece.

Leonardo da Vinci

(1452-1519)

www.bizzybeepublishing.biz

Reprinted in 2008
Printed and bound in China

The cat always leaves a mark on his friend.

Aesop 6th century BC

But buds will be roses, and kittens, cats –
more's the pity!

Louisa May Alcott (1832-1888)

It's my cat's world. I merely open the cans.

Author Unknown

I've learned I can cat-proof my house,
But I can't cat-proof my heart.

Author Unknown,
from "Cat-Proofing"

To a dog you're family, to a cat you're staff.

Author Unknown

He is proud of the lustre of his coat, and cannot endure that a hair of it shall lie the wrong way.

Jules Champfleury (1821-1889)

There is no more intrepid explorer than a kitten.

Jules Champfleury (1821-1889)

Of course cats are smarter than dogs. It takes intelligence to be that devious and cruel!

Author Unknown

The cat lives alone.He has no need of society.

François René de Chateaubriand (1768-1848)

Puss, with delight
beyond expression,
Surveyed the scene
and took possession.

William Cowper
(1731-1800)

Blessed are those who love cats,
for they shall never be lonely.
Author Unknown

Every life should have nine cats.

Author Unknown

The purity of a person's heart can be quickly measured by how they regard cats.

Author Unknown

...cats, so strong and gentle,
the pride of the household...
Charles Baudelaire (1821-1867)

The cat... obeys only when she pleases... and scratches everything on which she can lay her paw.

François René de Chateaubriand
(1768-1848)

What greater gift than...

...the love of a cat?

Charles Dickens (1812-1870)

Until one has loved an animal, a part of one's soul remains unawakened.

Anatole France (1844-1924)

When I play with my cat,
who knows whether I do not make her
more sport than she makes me?

Michel Eyquem, seigneur de Montaigne (1533-1592)

I like little Pussy,
Her coat is so warm,

And if I don't hurt her
She'll do me no harm....

Mother Goose (fl. 18th century),
from "Little Pussy"

Once [a cat] has given its love, what absolute confidence, what fidelity of affection!

Theophile Gautier (1811-1872)

Who can believe that there is no soul behind those luminous eyes!

Theophile Gautier (1811-1872)

It's better to feed one cat than many mice.

Norwegian Proverb

When you feel that
all the world is against
you, the affection
of a little cat can
mean so much.

Author Unknown

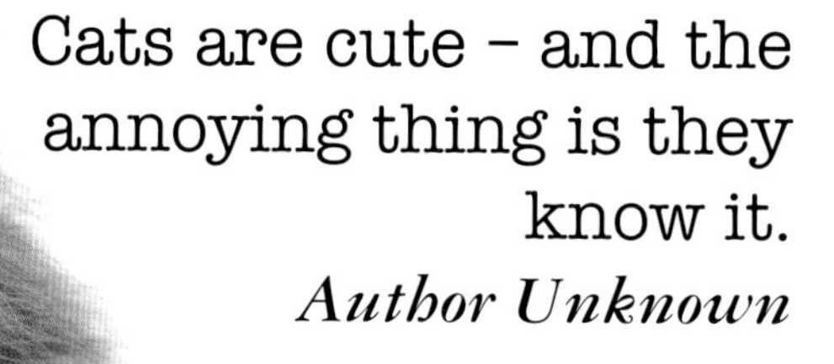

Cats are cute – and the annoying thing is they know it.

Author Unknown

To you it may look like
a beautiful new chair –
to a cat it's one big
scratch post.
Author Unknown

Cats' whiskers are so sensitive, they can find their way through the narrowest crack in a broken heart.

Author Unknown

Kittens believe that all nature is occupied with their diversion.

F.A. Paradis de Moncrif (1687-1770)

Everything that moves, serves to interest and amuse a cat.

F.A. Paradis de Moncrif (1687-1770)

No matter how much the cats fight, there always seem to be plenty of kittens.

Abraham Lincoln
(1809-1865)

[A kitten] does not discover that her tail belongs to her until you tread on it.
Henry David Thoreau (1817-1862))

[A kitten] gets himself into every kind of trouble....

Jules Champfleury (1821-1889)

Dogs remember faces, cats places.

English Saying

The cat is nature's Beauty.

French Proverb

Cats can never be fully domesticated – prowling the suburban street they are as wild as a leopard in the savannah.

Author Unknown

Nobody can give a withering stare quite as crushing as a disdainful cat.

Author Unknown

Cat: A pygmy lion who loves mice,
hates dogs, and patronizes human beings.

Oliver Herford (1863-1935)

Is there anything quite as expressive as a cat's tail? Kinked or straight it tells the story of a hundred moods.

Author Unknown

In Chinese legend the cat inherited dignity from its mother, the lioness, and curiosity and playfulness from its father, the monkey.

If stretching were wealth, the cat would be rich.

African Proverb

[Cats] are the cleanest, cunningest, and most intelligent things I know....
Mark Twain (1835-1910)

It is difficult to obtain the friendship of a cat. It is a philosophic animal... and one that does not place its affections thoughtlessly.

Theophile Gautier (1811-1872)

Those who will play
with cats must expect
to be scratched.
Miguel de Cervantes
(1547-1616)

[A cat] will make itself the companion of your hours of work, of loneliness, or of sadness.

Theophile Gautier (1811-1872)

To others she
may seem just
a common
little moggy,
but to me she
is my friend,
confidante
and comfort.

Aubtor Unknown

Is there anything
as beautiful as a
cat's eyes?
Jewel-like they
captivate the
heart.

Aubtor Unknown

If animals could speak... the cat would have the rare grace of never saying a word too much.

Mark Twain (1835-1910)

If man could be crossed with the cat, it would improve man, but it would deteriorate the cat.

Mark Twain (1835-1910)

The cat is mighty dignified...

until the dog comes by.

Southern Folk Saying

In ancient times
cats
were worshipped
as gods

they have never forgotten this.

Author Unknown

...let me not forget
that chairs were put
on earth to shred;
and what I like to call
a lap is actually a
cat-bed.

Author Unknown, from
"I'm Only Human"

Kiss me little kitty
and let me be your friend
If by chance you scratch me
don't worry it will mend
Love me little kitty
and play with me a while
I know you don't like cuddles
it just isn't your style

Author Unknown

Sometimes he sits...
looking into your face with an expression so gentle and caressing that the depth of this gaze startles you.

Theophile Gautier (1811-1872)

You know you're cat obsessed when you sleep in the spare room – because your cats have taken over your bed.

Author Unknown

There's no crime from which a cat can't extricate itself by a little timely purring.

Author Unknown

...he is of the tribe of Tiger.

Christopher Smart (1722-1771)
"on his cat Jeoffrey", from Jubilate Agno

A little drowsing cat is an image of perfect beatitude.

Jules Champfleury (1821-1889)

If you put a cat in a hat she will not forgive you that. She's elegant, refined and cool, so please don't make her play the fool.

Author Unknown

We hope that you have enjoyed this book, but please remember that owning a cat, or any pet, is a serious commitment. Animals need lots of love and attention, so please look after your pet responsibly.

The publisher would like to thank Warren Photographic for the use of their photographs.